What if . . .

Volume 2

By: Connie Smith

First Edition

By Connie Smith

© 2017 by Connie Smith

Edited by Carlie Mae and Lilly Sherman

ISBN: 978-1-365-76713-5

Table of Contents

Chapter	Page

iv

Dedication

Firstly, I dedicate this book to my loving husband Dean. Without him, I could not do what I do; nor would I be where I am in spirit without his strong love and belief in me and in my walk.

Secondly, I dedicate this book to Denise Anderegg, who has been a wonderful friend for a very long time. She has so encouraged me and strengthened me. And, like my husband, she has believed in me for many long years. Without these two people (and others as well), I would not be where I am today in my understanding of spiritual things. Thank you both so very much.

Prologue

This is my fourth book that God's Spirit has inspired me to write. I am not the typical author who can just sit down and make up something to entertain the reading-audience. Many authors *can*, and it is a true *gift* to be able to do so. And I wish that I *could* do my writing with such ease. However, I am in a very *different* place as an author: Sometimes I have to wait a long time between books, while at other times, I can write another book immediately after publishing a project. For example, this book (*What If . . . Volume 2*) came on the heels of *What If . . . Volume 1*: I completed it while my editors were still working on volume 1. That is how God's Spirit works in my life.

This book is true; every single incident happened. And it is for people who have open minds with teachable spirit. I am being very *daring* with what I will try to convey to the readers. The events in this book are some of my most precious moments with my great and awesome God! The words are very deep: They are the spiritual things that I learned as I waited on the Lord.

I hope and pray that the reading-audience will appreciate my *openness* in sharing my experiences in the spirit. If my audience should *not* share my wonder, awe, and appreciation of my experiences, I will love and appreciate my audience anyway!

I have had many experiences in the realm of spiritual learning, and I give credit to all my teachers who encouraged me. I have heard and have seen many spiritual things; and in every case, they were presented to me directly from the Spirit of God.

In this book, I will do my best to explain some of the spiritual things that I have learned. Unfortunately, however, spiritual experiences are extremely difficult to record, for words seem to *weaken* the power of the experience.

I did not *create* any of the spiritual experiences in this book; I only *recorded* them so that those with eyes could see and those with ears could hear what the Spirit conveyed to me.

Chapter 1: The Beginning - Intuition

As I mentioned in my previous book titled *What if . . . Volume 1*, I was very young when I first became aware of certain things without anyone *telling* me about them. I had a knowing, called *intuition*, at a young age.

Have you ever had a feeling where you *knew* something about someone or something without anyone *telling* you? I have had *many* such feelings.

For example, I can remember *one* experience where I *knew* something which I had no *reason* to know, except for the voice of the Spirit of God. I had my *children* with me downtown one day, trying to find new clothes for them for the upcoming school

1

year. And suddenly, I just *knew* that someone was at the front door of our house looking to visit us. Hence, I spoke it out to the children, whereupon they asked me:

"Mom, how do you know that?"

I replied:

"I don't *know* how I know it. I just know that someone is trying to *visit* us."

Apparently, the Spirit of *God* had spoken the message into my *own* spirit.

Later, when we got home, we saw a note that was written by the person who had tried to visit us. And it confirmed the time when I had told the children about someone being at the house, trying to visit us.

I had many *more* such incidents. I would be away from home, and I would know that someone was trying to *telephone* us. These incidents were happening to me long before the days of *answering machines*, and I always learned later that someone *had* tried to reach us by telephone.

Sometimes the incidents concerned people whom I could trust and whom I should *not* trust. And what I learned (from the incidents) protected me many times during my lifetime, both during my *childhood* and during my *adult* years. I am so *grateful* for the voice of the Spirit of God: More than once, I was protected from being molested or raped, because I listened and obeyed that "knowing." I could always feel it in the pit of my stomach. Many times, I would feel *tense*, and I would know that I could not be around certain people.

For instance, I had an incident in elementary school. When I was nine or ten years old, I used to visit a classmate. I would play with her after supper, and I would always feel a "tension" around her father (i.e., the *intuitive* feeling that I discussed earlier).

Nothing ever happened between the girl's father and me. But later, it became common knowledge that he *had* done bad things to one *other* girl, and they were the kind of things that I knew he would have done with *me* if he had had the opportunity.

At another time, I experienced a *similar* situation, and the voice of the Spirit *again* saved me from a terrible fate. We must always listen, listen, listen to our inner voice, which is the Voice of God that is trying to protect us.

This voice is the voice of the Spirit that I have followed all my life. And to this day, I watch others associate with certain people whom I know well. But because of my inner voice, I would never trust those "certain people" *anywhere*, not even in a *church*.

We must make our own walk; we must *never* follow the crowd just to be popular. It is so *dangerous* today. That is why we all are equipped with the voice of spirit at birth, and we must learn to *listen* to it.

I am much older now, and I *still* listen and pay attention to my inner voice. I always will.

Chapter 2: Married with Children

When I was growing up, people married young, and so did my husband and I. He was 19½ and I was 16½ years old. We both were reared with a lot of responsibility, and that is why our marriage worked.

I had my first child when I was almost 19; I had my second child the following year; and I had my last child 26 months later. During this period, I had a lot of opportunity to listen to the Voice of God's Spirit, and I am so grateful for the Spirit's leading.

Without any hint, input, or evidence from the children, I often knew when they were doing things that they should *not* be doing. And they would ask me if I had eyes in the back of my head.

Many would argue that my ability was nothing more than a mother's intuition, but I beg to differ: It was the Voice of God letting me know where the children were.

I caught and confronted my children many times when they were into mischief. One time, I was working in the *boys'* room, and we recently had bought a *desk* for them to use for their homework. And I happened to be walking past the desk when I heard the voice of the Spirit telling me to open a certain drawer. I obeyed, and I was *shocked* when I saw some pictures from a *Playboy Magazine*.

Then, when the boys came home, I showed them what I had discovered in their desk, and they wanted to fall through the floor in shame. I questioned them and learned that one of their classmate's *father* subscribed to the magazine, and he did not throw away the old issues. And when the boys would visit their classmate, they would end up in a small shed where the old magazines were stored. Evidently, the classmate's father permitted the boys to keep some of the magazines.

At another time, I was going to the mailbox when I went past our older son's car, and I heard the Voice of the Spirit say:

"Look under the front seat."

Hence, I opened the door; I slid my hand under the seat; and I found *more* things that shocked me. Naturally, I again confronted my son, and he *again* was embarrassed at what I had discovered.

I am positive that both boys were extremely happy to move out of the house when they grew up. But even after they had move out, I still would know if they were into mischief. The Voice of God, with which we are born, is a wonderful thing.

Chapter 3: Another Door Opens

After the children grew up, I had more time to think about spiritual things, and I began to be aware of the presence of those who had gone over to the "other side."

I remember that, after my grandmother (on my mother's side) passed away, I often would feel her spirit all around me.

Before her death, she was so happy when I went to the hospital to deliver our daughter, and she asked the nurses if she could hold the baby. It just so happened that our daughter was the first girl born into our family in several generations, and so

Grandma was very pleased to see and hold her extra-special grandchild.

Sadly, my grandmother died shortly after my daughter's birth, and her spirit was present in my life for many years. I am sure that she watched my child grow. At that time in my life, I would *feel* (the presence of those who had passed on) more often than I would *see* them. But that would change.

My father's health began to fail when he was in his 60's. He got up one morning and could no longer speak, so it was obvious that he had suffered a *stroke* during the night. But at the time, my parents had no insurance, and Medicare was not yet a part of our lives; and therefore, nothing was done about my father's condition.

Soon after, my father began to behave very differently. For example, he began to experience *mood-swings*. He always had been a very mild, quiet man, and he now would become *angry*. Once, he even *hit* my mom, which was so *opposite* of his normal self. And after such episodes, he suddenly would realize what he had done, and he would *apologize* for his actions.

At the time, we never had heard of *Alzheimer's Disease*, and so we just kept loving him and overlooking his actions as much as we could. My father also had *Colon Cancer*, and he had a *colostomy* surgery, which altered his life *completely*. After the surgery, he was not sociable at all.

My father never healed properly from the last surgery, and he developed "bleeders," which are tiny blood vessels that become irritated and can bleed into the colostomy bag. And my mother would have to do so much *clean-up* work whenever the bleeders would bleed.

My mother suffered *greatly* with her knees, for both were badly worn and needed replacing. And unfortunately, my father's condition left her with a lot of *washing*, but she held on because of the *love* that they shared.

Finally, my father developed *Sundowner Syndrome*: He would go to bed and *wake up* after a short time, believing that he had slept the entire night. And he would keep Mom up night-and-day.

Eventually, Mom had to place him in a *nursing home*, and because of his *temper*, he had to be medicated with *tranquilizer* to keep him calm.

I visited my father many times, but we could not communicate, for he had lost his faculty to speak. Therefore, I would hug him and tell him how much I loved him, and he would *smile* at me. Through my intuition, I felt that he believed that I was one of the *aides* who cared for him.

Before long, my father showed a steady decline in his physical appearance, and he began to lose control of his bodily functions. And by the time of his death, he had reverted to the *fetal* position, and he weighed about 120 pounds. (His normal weight was 210 lbs.)

When he finally passed away, his death shocked *all* of us, but I also was so relieved, for he had no quality of life.

I already had wept for him for many years as I watched his spirit leave while his body was slowly dying. Therefore, I felt no guilt for feeling relieved when he died.

My father passed away 23-25 years ago, possibly even longer; and I loved him deeply. I was closer to him than I was to my mother, and I knew that he likewise loved *me* very much.

My parents were married for 63 years when my father passed away.

Chapter 4: My Father's Visit from the Other Side

One evening, I was sitting in the living room after my husband had retired for the night. And suddenly, my father, in spirit form, walked into the room.

Yes, I saw him with my *eyes;* I did not see him just in my mind. He was about 30 years old, strong, handsome as ever, and he had a full head of hair that was dark as usual with natural waves in it. He looked *wonderful*, and I recognized him at once. He had a big smile, and he greeted me with the usual "hello" like the way he did when he was alive.

I watched him sit down in a chair, and after a few seconds, he said:

> "I have come to tell you some things that you don't know, but they will help you in the future.
>
> Just like on Earth, the other side has levels of education. It has schools that have different levels of *understanding*.
>
> When I first went to the other side, I was placed in a 'school of forgiveness' for about a week. Before my death, I had held grudges against *many* people, and I had to *empty* all the grudges by *forgiving* those who had victimized me.
>
> Next, I was sent to a 'school for love.' We don't *know* what love is in the physical world.
>
> I, then, was put to work at all the things that had excited me when I was alive.

Now, I am having a *wonderful* time where I live: I do all the things that I had loved to do when I was on the earth.

The other side is *not* what we have been told; it is so much *better*. There is no one sitting and playing the harp, and there are no golden streets. *None* of those things is desired or needed on the other side.

Read the *Book of Revelation* and know that it is *inside* of us, not in the *physical* realm. When we go there, we have no need of sleep, money, pills, or *any* of the things that we need here. We have no mansions in the physical, for *we* are the house of God. *We* are His dwelling place as it reads in the Scripture. 1 Corinthians 3:16 reads, 'Know ye not that ye are the temple of God, and that the Spirit of God dwelleth in you?' (King James Version).

I never get hungry, tired, or sick, because I am no longer physical. And I don't need a *house*, for the weather is *perfect* all the time.

All the colors on the other side are *intensified*: They are much brighter, more intense, and deeper in their hues. They are so *delightful*.

I am never sad or depressed, and no one ever *cries* on the other side."

My father stayed a long time and spoke of many other things before leaving. I did not completely understand everything that he told me, but I know that he was telling the truth.

After the visit, I began to research the things that my father's spirit had told me.

Some may think that I do not believe in Heaven, but this is not true. I *do* believe in Heaven, but not in the way that we all have learned from traditional sources. There are *other* dimensions and realms of Glory.

I have come to a great *peace* at what is happening on the other side. My father's description of the other side is so much better than any other explanation that I ever have heard.

If you want to understand deeper things, the book *The Revealing Word*, by Charles Fillmore, is tremendous for opening your understanding to the spiritual look at many things. Below is a direct quote from that book on the "many mansions" of John 14:2,

> "<u>Degrees of Realization of the Truth of Being</u>. The 'place' that Jesus prepared is a definite state of realization of truth into which may come all who take up the same denials and affirmations that He took up."

Before I ever read this, I knew and had seen (by the Spirit) that it was *not* what I had been taught by the ministers whom I had sat under for many years. And my father had come to *confirm* many things that I already had seen.

The Lord is so *wonderful* to all of us. When we already have seen something by His Spirit, He confirms, over and over, that it is the truth.

Chapter 5: My Search to Confirm the Message

5a: Wisdom

I found several passages in the Scripture that concern *wisdom*. We must remember that "tree of life" in the second passage below (Proverbs 3:18) symbolizes wisdom:

> "Happy is the man that findeth Wisdom, and the man that getteth understanding, for the merchandise of it is better than the merchandise of silver, and the gain of it thereof than fine gold." (Proverbs 3:13-14)

> "She is a tree of life to them that lay hold upon her: and happy is every

one that retaineth her." (Proverbs 3:18)

"Doth not wisdom cry? And understanding put forth her voice?" (Proverbs 8:1)

"Wisdom has builded her house, she has hewn out her 7 pillars:" (Proverbs 9:1)

Obviously, the Scripture considers wisdom to be extremely valuable, even more valuable than pure *gold*.

Incidentally, the "tree of life" is also mentioned in the *Book of Revelation* (three times), and the words "gold" and "golden" are mentioned *20* times.

Interestingly, many believe that Heaven has streets of pure gold, which suggests that Heaven has *limitless* amount of gold. And hence, some may conclude that gold must be *important* in Heaven.

However, for whatever it's worth, Revelation 21:21 mentions only *one* street that is made of pure gold:

> "And the twelve gates were twelve pearls: every several gate was of one pearl: and the street of the city was pure gold, as it were transparent glass." (Revelation 21:21)

In any event, when I began to research the words that the Voice of God's Spirit had spoken to me, I knew that He was showing me some deep truths. It is all about a deep inner work in the *consciousness*.

Some may say:

> "It is not in the Scripture where people, who have *died*, came back and *spoke* to anyone."

Well, I disagree: I say that the Scripture *does* mention such people! For example, concerning the death-and-resurrection of Jesus, the Bible reads:

"And behold, the veil of the temple was rent in twain from the top to the bottom; and the earth did quake, and the rocks rent; and the graves were opened; and many bodies of the saints which slept arose, and came out of the graves after his resurrection, and went into the holy city and appeared unto many." (Matthew 27:51-53)

In the *Book of John*, chapters 20 and 21, Jesus appeared to different people, speaking and eating and giving instructions. So, when that "veil" was rent (or, torn) into two pieces from the top to the bottom, showing that the way was made into the very inner recesses of your own *self*, the house of God and those on the other side were given access to *us* as well as we to *them*. Jesus made the way! It is all *open* now!

5b: Heaven

I wonder how many people have ever thought about what it would be like to live in *Heaven*. As for me, if Heaven were anything like what I learned about it as a child, it would be *boring*: At one time, I owned three harps: an autoharp, an Angel Harp, and an Indian Harp (Native American); and it would not be lovely for me to sit on some cloud and play a *harp* all day! I am a person of movement and action, and I sure don't want to be where I can't move and do something *useful*. Some people have a lazy nature and would *love* to spend their entire lives doing nothing, but I am not *built* that way. I love to work. So, sitting on a cloud and playing the harp all day would not be Heaven for me.

5c: My Father's Spirit

My father's spirit remains close to me, and it is around me all the time. I feel his presence; and to show me that he is around, I find coins in the strangest places. And every time I do, I say:

"Hello Dad, how *are* you today?"

I receive *comfort* from him, and I know that he has helped me in *many* ways to obtain some things that had looked impossible. He has become like a guardian angel to me.

As I mentioned earlier, my father's spirit stayed a long time with me, and I never have forgotten what he told me. Since then, books have been placed in my path to confirm what he told me.

Everyone should read the book *Return from Tomorrow*, by George G. Ritchie, M.D. It was published by Chosen Books, Copyright 1978. And it is distributed by Word books. It is a book that I will never be without, for it helped me to open my mind to another way of seeing what happens after death. Read, read, read; it will help you to grow and answer your questions.

The best book that I ever read concerning the *Book of Revelation* is by Zachary Landsdowne. His book is titled *The Revelation of Saint John,* and it is marketed by Weiser Books, ISBN: 1-57863-342-7. The author has taken the book verse-by-verse and has broken it down. I found it to be profound and true. If you truly want to understand the *Book of Revelation,* this book will help you. It will be worth every dime to purchase it.

What if a loved one should appear to each of *us?*

Chapter 6: A New Work; A Greater Revelation

6a: The Harps

Sometime after my father's visit from the other side, another wonderful experience opened for me. My husband and I had spent many years in ministry, and I felt a call to visit and minister at a small place in Missouri, where we had visited many times.

While we were there, a woman asked me to teach her how to play an autoharp, because she knew that I had played the autoharp for over 40 years. And of course, I told her that I would be *happy* to teach her.

Then, one evening after dinner, my husband Dean and I went to the woman's home to give her the first autoharp lesson. We did the lesson in her bedroom, and she learned quickly. She even learned enough for us to play some *songs* together. And when we had finished playing, she asked:

"Have you ever seen an *Angel Harp*?"

I thought for a moment and answered:

"No, I haven't."

The woman went to her closet and brought out the most beautiful harp that I have ever seen. It was the same *size* as the autoharp, but that was where the similarities ended. The Angel Harp was all white, and it had beautiful pictures of *angels* on it. It was *breathtaking* to see. I was so awed and *excited* about it. I asked:

"Where did you *get* it? What does it *sound* like? How do you *play* it?"

She strummed across it, and it produced a *heavenly* sound. She explained that there was nothing to *press*, like on an *autoharp*. You just play it any way you want to play. She, then, asked me if *I* would like to play it.

I told her that I didn't know how, whereupon the woman showed me how to play it. And I fell in *love* with the instrument.

The woman explained that she had attended a meeting where the group meditated to the music of the Angel Harp. And she went places in the Holy Spirit where she never had gone before.

Interestingly, she had purchased the harp at the *meeting*, and it had remained in her closet until she received her first *lesson* from me.

In any event, the woman asked me the most shocking question:

"Would you like to *have* it?"

I asked:

"How much *is* it?"

She replied:

> "No, it wouldn't cost you *anything*. I would give it to you for teaching me how to play the *autoharp*. I know that you would use it more than *I* would."

Of course, I was *overwhelmed* by her gifting me with such a beautiful and costly instrument. At the time, its value was somewhere around $1000.00.

I didn't have a *clue* as to why I was receiving this harp or how I would use it in my life. I was certain of one thing only: There were (and still are) many doors in the spirit world that I never had opened; and perhaps, this was just one more door for me to open.

Anyway, a short time later, we felt a call to go to Ohio, where we had ministered to a certain group many times before. We always stayed with a special couple, and they were excited that we were coming.

Coincidentally, the lady (i.e., our host) recently had been gifted with an "Indian Harp," which is used for the same purposes as the Angel Harp. Both harps are used for meditation and therapy. (The word "therapy" means, "a treatment to relieve or heal a disorder.")

My friend (the host) had a fear of tuning her harp. So, I brought out my tuning equipment and set out to show her how to tune a harp. I have been tuning harps for many years, and it is vital to have a sensitive touch with the tuning keys. Otherwise, the strings could *break*.

I placed the harp on the kitchen table and began my task. The harp was *lovely*, and as I was trying to explain what I was doing, my friend was standing a few feet away near the *sink*, and she said:

> "Take the harp *home* with you, for I would be *afraid* to ever do what you are doing."

I asked:

> "What did you say?"

She repeated her statement, and I asked:

> "Are you *sure*?"

She answered:

> "Yes, I will never *use* it, and you *will*."

At the time, I had no idea as to how my two new, very-awesome harps would be used in my life. But I knew that, without *question*, my Creator was getting ready to do something *overwhelming* in my life.

The Indian Harp was even more costly than the *Angel Harp.* It was made of real Redwood, which is not cheap at all. So, now in my possession, I had well over $2,000.00 in harps, and I had no clue as to why I even *had* them.

Let me give some details about these two harps that I received as gifts. They were developed through a revelation that was given to a woman named Rev. Barbie Edwards in Colorado.

As I already have mentioned, the Indian Harp (i.e., Native American) is made of Redwood. It is very beautiful, and it plays in a *minor* key

On the other hand, the Angel Harp is white, and it is decorated with figures of angels. It plays beautifully in a *major* key.

Both harps were (and still are) prayed over before they were sold, and a spirit guide was sent with each harp to guide whoever would own it. And after the acquisition of the harps, I worked with both spirit guides in every session that I attended.

6b: Vibrational Sound Healing

Both the Angel Harp and the Indian Harp were created for meditation, but they also are excellent for clearing blockages in a person through "Vibrational Sound Healing." This type of healing is a very old and simple method which is a tool for healing that is completely natural. It is very useful in clearing emotional blockages. These blockages are made up of emotional thought-patterns and old belief-structures. They cause tension in the *mind* like a cold draft or an injury causes muscular tension in the *body*. These emotional blockages resist consciousness and require higher vibration to break this vicious cycle. (*Sound Healing with the Five Elements*, by Daniel Perret.)

Since sound is non-physical, we need to understand that the body can be restored to balance through non-physical means. Vibrational Sound Healing works with the energy fields of the body. Energy fields exist around *everything* in the world, including humans. And vibrations, from certain harps and other instruments, can *penetrate* these energy fields. Therefore, such vibrations can be used to *neutralize* energy disturbances that are caused by emotional blockages.

Music affects people in different ways: It can *elevate* the spirit; it can *depress* us; and it can *inspire* us. The use of sound for healing-purposes is a re-emerging technique-and-science that is based on Sympathetic Vibratory physics. The science of sound-healing existed in the past. The ancients used tools such as the Tibetan singing-bowls, drums, and the Australian aborigine didgeridoos. They, once, were *lost* to us, but this technology is now resurging.

Note: Didgeridoo -- musical instrument made from a long wooden tube that produces a low, drone sound.

Chapter 7: Understanding the New Work

7a: The Harps

After I returned home and realized that I was the proud owner of two harps with which I didn't know what to do, I prayed for direction. And soon after, a friend came for a visit. She inquired about the harps and said:

> "*Place* them on me, and I will tell you if they feel *good* or not."

I followed her instruction and waited. We both had our eyes closed, and I strummed the Indian Harp first and then followed with the Angel Harp. She had a vision with both harps, and so did I. We discussed what we saw, and she went home soon after.

I was *intrigued* with the vision that I had experienced, and so I *prayed* about it.

What if each of *us* should receive a new therapy to do and the tools to *do* it?

Little by little, people came to visit me, and many times, they would ask me to lay the *harps* on them. And we both would see things in the spirit.

I had been doing therapeutic massage for many years, so I had the table and the equipment for people to use along with the harps. Soon, a pattern began to develop on how to use them. And before long, I had a clientele building and was seeing some good healings taking place. I was led by God's Spirit, one step at a time, until I fully understood what the work was about. I learned how to test the energy centers of the body (the Chakras) for activity or *non*-activity; I learned how to bring in Essential Oils for part of the healing; and I learned many other things as I was so directed.

7b: Essential Oils

I can almost hear some curious people thinking:

"What is an Essential Oil?"

Essential oils are some of the oldest and most powerful therapeutic agents known. They are made from certain plants' leaves when they are mature. The leaves are harvested; they are pressed; the oils of the leaves are separated from any other kind of fluid; and the oils are processed, bottled, and sold for health purposes.

Essential oils have been used for anointing and for curing every ailment known to humans. They were widely used by the Egyptians for purification and for embalming.

Many essential oils have antiviral, anti-inflammatory, anti-bacterial, and therapeutic effect along with hormonal and even *psychological* effects. (*Essential Oils Desk Reference*). Hence, many essential oils, such as clove and lemon, were used for antiseptics long before the discovery of germ killers.

The essential oils helped so many who came to me for therapy. Their smells are also used in "Aromatherapy." As I would apply the oil, many would *weep* as their therapy would begin, even before I had placed the *harps* on them.

I have seen many miracles in my vibrational work. I was directed by the Creator to mix *oils* for people, and I watched them bloom by their wearing the special oil.

As for the harps, I used them for breaking down psychological walls of the minds.

7c: Totem Animals

After a while, I developed an information form for my clientele. I had every person, who came for Vibrational Sound Therapy, fill it out and sign it before beginning any type of treatment. And within a short time, the Spirit would give me the procedure for the method of treatment.

On the first day of treatment, I would have a time of *counseling* with the clients to get to know them. Meanwhile, I already would have looked up their names and birth dates before their arrival, which would have given me a lot of *information* about them. And I would do a lot of *praying* over the names; and many times, I would receive much information from the Spirit before the clients' arrival.

When potential clients would call for an appointment, I would ask them pertinent questions: Why are you seeking this therapy? Do you believe in past lives? Are you open to learn-and-see new things? . . . If I would feel that the applicants were not teachable, I would not accept them.

At first, I accepted *all* applicants. And before long, I had *completely* worn myself out on some of those who were not serious. As for those who *were* serious and teachable, they were healed and helped greatly, thanks be to the Spirit!

Many times, in the process of laying on the harps and having a whole dimension of the spirit world open to me, I would receive what the clients' "totem" would be.

Some may remark:

> "*Totem*? Never heard of it. What *is* it?"

A "totem" is an animal or a natural object that is assumed as the symbol of a group, a clan, or a family. For example, in front of their villages, many Native Americans had a wooden post with several *animal-heads* carved on it, each animal representing a tribe, a clan, a family, etc.

In any event, I see many of our health problems in a way that is quite easy to understand. I believe that we suffer most of our sicknesses because we have lost our touch with nature and with the animals. We have *modernized*, which means that everything around us is cement, black top, or plastic. And we don't get enough sunshine, fresh air, or *movement* in our lives.

Furthermore, we have occupied the animals' *homes*, and we wonder why they *annoy* us, but we are actually annoying *them*. Animals have different diets, different habitats, and different ways of taking care of their young. But they are very much like

people in their diversity. For instance, some animals

are better mothers than *other* animals. The otter has

a fantastic *playful* nature. The wolves run in packs

and have a very complex *social* order, while other

animals are *loners*.

When a client would come to me for

Vibrational Sound Therapy, I would see an animal in

the *spirit*. And when the harps were played, I would

either *see* a totem or receive a *message* from the

totem, for every animal that crosses our path has

something to say. If a certain animal should show up

over-and-over in our lives, it must have a special

meaning.

Some of my friends have told me that a bird

had shown up and had looked at them as if it wanted

to *say* something. And my clients and I, likewise,

have had such experience(s), which suggests that animals and humans are spiritually *connected*.

I know that I personally have two totems: the giraffe and the snowy owl. And if I look up these two animals, they fit me to a T.

What if each of *us* could see what totem animal we are?

For more information on totem animals, read the books below:

- *Animal-Speak: The Spiritual and Magical Powers of Creatures Great and Small.* (by Ted Andrews)
- *Animal-Wise: The Spirit Language and Signs of Nature.* (by Ted Andrews)
- *Animal-Speak Pocket Guide.* (by Ted Andrews)

- *Animal Spirit Guides.* (by Steven D. Farmer, Ph.D.)

I pray that you will invest in these books and find *your* totem animal. If you pray and ask God to *show* you, He *will*.

Chapter 8: The Spirit Help Arrives

8a: <u>Spirits</u> <u>of</u> <u>the</u> <u>Chiefs</u>

By now, I had owned the Angel Harp and the Indian Harp for about a year. And the clients and I were receiving *visions* from God's Spirit when the harps were played. During every session, I would receive *insight* from the Holy Spirit as to the *meaning* of the many things that the client and I were seeing in the vision(s).

On one occasion, a client called and came to see me, and when I placed the Indian Harp on her, I had a vision. We both were meditating with our eyes closed when the vision occurred. I was shown by the Spirit that, along a certain wall, there were some

Indian Chiefs' *spirits*. And three of the spirits spoke to me:

> "I am Geronimo, chief of the Bedonkohe Chiricahua Mescalero Apache."

> I am Chief Joseph, chief of the Wallamotkin (Wallowa) Nez Perce."

> I am Red Cloud, chief of the Oglala Lakota (Teton) Sioux. We have heard this harp and have come to see what you are doing."

These three spirits were standing with their arms folded over their chest, and they were looking very *seriously* at me. But I felt no fear, because I knew that they had come to *help* me.

After the vision, the chiefs' spirits would show up at every session, and they would tell me if the client had been in their tribe when they (the spirits) were alive. Sometimes, the chiefs' spirits would

49

bring many *other* spirits with them who would perform special dances to help the client or to show an *emotion* for him (or, her).

Later, the spirit of Sitting Bull (medicine chief and holy man of the Hunkpapa Teton [Lakota] Sioux) showed up, and he would bring Native American *medicine* into the room.

Every session was different, but the spirits of the three chiefs would be with me during every session from their first appearance onward.

I have always had a heart for the Native American people, and I love them more now than ever. What an awesome way of life they enjoyed, and what wonderful *wisdom* they had.

What if each of *us* should have a visit from the old chiefs and warriors?

8b: Angel Aquarius

One day, I was *praying* when I had a vision of a huge angel dressed in a beautiful blue gown. And she was so large that she filled the entire *house*. I asked:

"Who are you?"

She replied:

"My name is Aquarius."

I immediately contested her reply:

"That's a *Zodiac* sign, not a *name*."

She changed her tone of voice and said:

"My name is *Aquarius!* I should know my own *name!*"

I apologized at once, whereupon she told me that she was the angel over the Great Lakes, and she firmly informed me that she *does not* do rivers. She explained that she uses two bridges to begin her ascent: the Mackinac Bridge that connects Sault Ste. Marie, Michigan to Sault Ste. Marie, Ontario (Canada) and the Blue Water Bridge that connects Port Huron, Michigan to Point Edward, Ontario (Canada). I am sure that she can ascend from *anywhere*, but she was so wonderful to give me such details.

She became my loyal friend, and she would appear every time that I had a client.

8c: Angel Aurelia

A short time after my first vision of Angel Aquarius, I was treating a very dear friend of mine, and God's Spirit showed me a glorious *new* angel, who was working around my friend's body. The angel wore a gown whose color was *pinkish lavender*, a type of color that I never had *seen* before. And with her hands, the angel was sending out a

substance that looked *silvery*, and I spoke out to my
friend:

> "There is a new *angel* here today.
> She is not speaking, but she is
> working around your body with a
> silvery substance."

I, then, asked the angel for her name, and she
replied:

> "My name is Aurelia, and I mend
> peoples' *auras*."

Most of us know that an aura is the surrounding
energy of a person that provides *protection* in many
ways. But unfortunately, it becomes full of *holes*
when we get angry, when we have surgery, or when
we get upset.

Anyway, my friend felt so much *better* after
Angel Aurelia had healed her aura. And from this
vision forward, Aurelia would appear whenever I
would use the harps, and she would successfully heal

the client's *aura*. She would heal them in many ways, and I learned so much by just *watching* her.

I am now retired, but I think *often* of Angel Aquarius and Angel Aurelia, for they are *real,* and they even occasionally *visit* me. All this information was given to me by God's Spirit.

Chapter 9: What if an Angel Should *Visit* Us?

I believe that *many* people have seen the spirits of loved ones who had died, and most of them had no one with whom to share their experience: We are always so *afraid* of what others will think.

When people would come to me, they knew that it would be safe for them to speak to me, for I would understand. I have heard many stories of appearances of spirits of loved ones, appearances of angels, and stories of spirits who appeared to *assist* someone. All such encounters are always the intervention of *spiritual* help. The natural mind cannot *understand* these things, and we don't *have* to; we are just *grateful* for the help.

I have heard many stories concerning the spirit world. For example, a lady told me that some *flowers* had moved after a funeral, and no one in the natural had moved them. Another lady told me that a *lamp* would often turn on without anyone touching the switch. Someone even had a *message* on her answering machine when she arrived home, which was nothing unusual. But the caller had *died* three days earlier. Such stories seem to be everywhere. There are so many angels and spirits who help us every day, and we usually are not aware of their help. Every bit of information that I received was all from the Spirit of God.

What if each of *us* should see those on the other side?

I know that the people on the other side help *me* all the time. For instance, I needed some hanging-files. Therefore, my husband and I went to a sale, and my husband spotted a regular grocery bag that contained some *hanging-files*. The price was $2.00. Then, when we got home, I found 30 brand new hanging-files in the bag; what a buy! How we ever saw them was only because of divine help.

At the same sale mentioned above, I was also looking for a variety of plastic containers, and I saw some for only $.50 and $.25 each! My husband and I have had so *many* such experiences in our walk in the spirit that they are *common* for us.

I read a book by Joel Goldsmith many years ago, and he said (I am paraphrasing):

> "Everything you will ever need is
> here now. There is no lack in
> having enough food, clothes,

gasoline, cars, houses, etc. To say
there is not enough is a lie."

I agree: I know that there is always enough if
you pay attention and handle things correctly. I was
raised by people who knew how to *stretch*
everything, and I am *grateful*.

Joel Goldsmith has helped me much to have an
open mind. He was such a wonderful man to follow
the voice within himself, and his books came when
my hunger got to the point where it *drew* them to me.
There is an old saying:

"When the student is ready, the
teacher shows up."

That has been so true in my life. And the
teacher can come in human form, in movie form, or
in book form. Most of my teachers have come in
book form, but when I first began my search, I did

have teachers in *human* form. Our Creator can put us in touch with whoever can help us in our search.

Chapter 10: Case 1 -- A Session with the Harps

I will share with you what I experienced during one of my sessions where the *harps* were used. This case involved an open-minded Jewish woman who was in her late 50's. And as with *all* my clients, I needed to gather some important *information* about her before I could start any treatment.

1. We talked about certain things: the client's *reason* for the treatment, what she *expected* from the treatment, etc.

2. I prayed and asked the Spirit of God for guidance on what *oils* to use.

3. I tested the client's "chakras" (or, *energy* centers) and learned that her *throat* chakra had some issues.

Therefore, I mixed an oil called "Free" and had the client apply it on her throat, after which her throat began to clear so that we could continue the session.

Then, I placed the Indian Harp on the client; we closed our eyes as I began to strum the harp; and we *meditated.*

I immediately had a vision and saw the Indian guide who was sent with the harp, and I could tell by his expression what he knew: The client had never been on my massage table before, and it was her first time with me for this kind of therapy.

The Indian guide stood over the client and remained in a meditative posture for a few minutes. Then, he straightened up; he pointed his arms straight ahead; and he made two small moves with his hands in a zig-zag-like motion. He, then, lowered his arms and looked straight ahead, which indicated that the client would travel in the right direction during her life. But down the road, she would experience a small "zig-zag" before continuing.

Now, the "zig-zag" did not mean that the client would encounter any kind of huge *bump* in her path, but just some *little* problems to work out. Life is *full* of change and bumps.

I could not see the *details* of the client's future problems; I merely *delivered* the message from the Spirit. But later, I learned that the Indian guide's prophecy proved to be true: The client *did* successfully work out some minor problems in her life.

Interestingly, the spirit of Apache Chief Geronimo (chief in the 1800's) said that the client had been a member of his tribe in her former life. And she was married to the same man to whom she was married in her *current* life. Sadly, the husband in her former life was killed in battle.

I saw that the client and her husband had not produced any children in their *former* life nor in their *current* life. Moreover, I received both of their Indian names as well as seeing that their marriage in *both* lives were *stormy*. I could see that they had to get back together during their *current* lifetime in attempt to take care of something that was still *unfinished* between them.

This same truth would come up during many other therapy sessions that involved other couples. They would end up marrying the same person over-and-over during many lifetimes to learn whatever lesson that the couple had not learned during their *earlier* lives.

We must learn the necessary lesson(s) so that our souls can progress and overcome our lower nature. When I say "lower nature," I mean the "natural man" part of us: The part in us that is selfish, ego-driven, lacking love, lacking patience, and lacking compassion for others. The earthen realm is our school to overcome and rise above fear, lust, impatience, hate, ignorance, and anything else that keeps us in selfish thinking.

I saw a group of Native Americans vigorously dancing around a fire. They danced in *one* direction and then danced in the *other* direction. They said that they were performing a dance of *change*. And shortly after, the client *would* experience a change in her life.

During the session, many *animals* made their appearance. And afterward, we went to Ted Andrews' *Animal-Speak Pocket Guide* and learned the *interpretation* for the animals.

The appearance of these animals gave the client a lot of comfort, direction, and answers to some of the questions that had been on her mind.

Under the *Angel Harp*, the client saw a huge angel with wings so large that they covered her *completely*. And I knew that it was *Angel Aquarius*, for she was always faithful to come and minister her loving touch to all my clients. Aquarius promised that, while she was staying in Michigan, she would hover over the client's residence and send down her power-and-love into the client's life.

Then, *Angel Aurelia* appeared and began to mend the client's aura. The client could feel the angel's touch as the angel worked around her. The aura was in such ragged state that it took a bit *longer* than usual to mend it, for Aurelia was very kind and *thorough* in her mending. And after the mending, Aurelia put a gold *sealing* around the aura, for it would be a better, stronger seal; and therefore, the aura would provide more *protection* for the location where the client would happen to be. At the time, the client and her husband were moving around frequently and staying with different relatives.

When Angel Aurelia had finished mending the client's aura, the client's *parents* showed up from the other side. They both had passed on many years earlier.

The mother began to apologize for her stubbornness toward the client when she was alive. She (the mother) had argued with her daughter about many things, and so their relationship had been a bit *rocky* at times. There was always *love* between them, but much disagreements as well. Hence, the mother had returned to ask for forgiveness and to give her love.

The father had come for *moral* support. He stood aside with 10 or 12 other family-members who had passed. I felt that they were grandparents, aunts, and uncles, and the client was greatly comforted by their presence.

I, then, saw the client when she was a child. She was a Jewish girl about seven or eight years old, and she was seated at a table in old Jerusalem on the Sabbath. She had the same mother and father as she had in her *current* life. Her father was reading the prayers and saying the proper things for the Sabbath Ceremony. The entire family was eating and drinking all the usual Sabbath foods and wine. The father lit the candles, and I felt deep *love* for the ceremony.

I felt my face light up with joy and excitement from the scene, and I felt as if I were the usual first one at the table on the day of Sabbath.

Then, the client spoke up and said that she still loves the ceremonies. She loves anything that involves the old rituals and ceremonies; they still make her excited. Her current deep love for such rituals and ceremonies came from her past life.

I saw that she wanted to be a *boy* back then, because the boys and men could *touch* the Torah and the other sacred objects. She would go to the Temple and be so *jealous* of the men and boys because of their privilege.

Interestingly, when the client was born (in her *current* life), her father insisted that she was a *boy*, and she would live as a *tomboy* during her childhood years. I believe that her being a tomboy was a *carryover* of her desire to be a boy during her *pas*t life.

At the very end of the session, I saw a crate of doves, and a *hand* appeared and opened the crate.

And when the door opened, many doves flew out to *freedom*. It seemed that the room was *full* of doves flying and wings flapping, and I felt that the release of the doves symbolized the great release of *peace* that the client had received. Doves represent *peace*, and the client had *imprisoned* her peace inside herself.

Before leaving, the client told me that she had *experienced* the release of peace that I had seen in the room. We both felt that our time together was a very blessed time in the Spirit of God.

Chapter 11: Case 2 -- Another Session with the Harps

This case involved a young lady who was only 18 years old, and her *parents* had purchased the session for her birthday. The client, even though very young, was very mature for her age, and she was very *sensitive* to the realm of spiritual things. She had *seen* and had *felt* some things for a long time. And she had a hungry heart and an open mind. She was a unique young person who had respect for her elders; she had integrity; she was knowledgeable; and she was exceptionally in tune with the session and with me.

During our pre-session discussion, the client admitted that (like *most* of us) she needed more *patience* in her life, which indicated that she was aware of her need for outside help.

I tested her chakras (energy centers) and found five of the seven major chakras to be fully active. And I did some therapy on the remaining two major chakras that were slightly blocked. We got them all working well before we started the session. (Some believe that we have as many as 114 chakras.)

I placed the Indian Harp on the client and strummed it. And the client said that it sounded as if a spiritual *being* were humming along with the harp. Moreover, she felt an authoritative *presence* on her left side. She believed that the presence was a Native American, but not one of the chiefs.

The client was correct: The Native American was *not* a chief. He was someone who had appeared to me during some earlier sessions. He called himself "The Indian of Reward" (from the Cheyenne Nation). And he had come with a basket that contained items that would be considered as gifts or rewards for the client.

This time, he had brought a pair of beautiful beaded *moccasins*, and he told us that the client's walk would be changing. She soon would be beginning a new walk.

The client said that something *already* had changed. She felt something *different* about her feet. Obviously, her physical body had responded to the spiritual gift.

Incidentally, during earlier sessions, the new moccasins had symbolized a change in the client's *thinking*, for as we walk, we also *think*. And therefore, the moccasins had represented *understanding*. But now, during the *current* session, the new moccasins had a *second* meaning.

Anyway, in addition to the new pair of moccasins, "The Indian of Reward" had brought a beautiful deer-hide fringed *dress* for the client, because clothing can represent new *wisdom*. For example, the Bible reads:

> "To appoint unto them that mourn in Zion, to give unto them beauty for ashes, the oil of joy for mourning, The garment of praise for the spirit of heaviness; . . ." (Isaiah 61:3)

> "For he put on righteousness as a breastplate and an helmet of salvation upon his head; and he put on the garments of vengeance for clothing, and was clad with zeal as a cloak." (Isaiah 59:17)

These passages symbolize a way of *thinking:* The garment of praise represents *joy*, and the garments of vengeance represent *anger* and a way of *balancing the score.*

Very soon, the young client would be heading for college, and her "wisdom-garment" would be changing.

At this point, some of the spiritual *animals* began to appear, and I later would explain the spiritual *meaning* of each of the animals and explain how they fit perfectly in *her* place in life. The Spirit knows what to *send* us to confirm everything that we see and hear.

I placed the *Angel Harp* on the client, whereupon my angel *helpers* began to appear. Angel Aquarius, the angel over the Great Lakes, appeared first. And she said that she was so *excited* to see such a young person who was so open to the spirit world. And she asked the client to say extra prayers for the situation concerning nuclear waste disposal.

The client had Catholic background, and so Aquarius asked her to say some "Hail Marys" in behalf of the nuclear waste problem. The client happily agreed.

Then, as the client began to tell me that she could see Aquarius' *wings*, Angel Aurelia (the healer of *auras*) made her appearance and did some work on the client's aura. Aurelia explained that, over the client's *heart* chakra, there was a *hole* due to some *hurts* that she had suffered. Aurelia did a special *sealing* on the client's aura, and therefore the client received a *healing* in her heart.

At the death of the client's grandfather, the client had not said good-bye to him. And the grandfather appeared during the session to let her know how *sorry* he was for not having said good-bye to *her*. He also told her that he had been around her many times; and she responded that she had *felt* his presence.

Additional spiritual beings had accompanied the grandfather, possibly the "other" grandparents and an aunt. They did not speak; they let the *grandfather* do all the talking, for he had some *things* to clear up with the client.

We then noticed some spiritual *birds* in the room, and we later would look up the *meaning* of each of them.

A few minutes later, the client's guardian angel "Sunny" appeared, and she was beautifully dressed in yellow. In the spirit world, colors have tremendous *iridescence*, and they always appear much more *vibrant*.

Angel Sunny stroked the client's hair and gave her much love. Sunny explained that she had been guiding the client's life ever since her birth.

Then, the Spirit showed me a former life of the client, who was a young girl approximately six or seven years old in Italy. Her name was Francesca, and she was from a poor family. She wore a peasant-style dress, and she was running through the streets in bare feet to get home, carrying a large loaf of *bread* tucked under her arm. She was in a hurry to get home, because her hungry family was waiting for her (and the bread) to get home for breakfast. Little Francesca had a serious look on her face, for she had been told not to loiter on the way.

After the vision, the client told me that she had *visited* Italy, and she felt so *comfortable* there. She had fallen in love with the country, and she wanted to visit it again.

The session had a positive *outcome* for the young client and me. I watched her as she entered adulthood and find a wonderful young man. She had such *wisdom* for her age, and she had such *connection* with the spiritual side of things. She was amazing; she was a joy to work with; and neither she nor I have forgotten the wonderful birthday present from her loving parents.

Chapter 12: Case 3 -- More Truths Learned

I would like to explain some deep information that I learned during one unusual session.

This case involved a female client who was in her 40's. When I placed the Indian Harp over her, the room filled with doves, and I knew immediately that we were seeing her *totem*. The vision had to do with her love of Mother Earth. When I spoke of what we were seeing, the client said that her favorite place was her backyard.

Then, the Indian guide appeared (i.e., the guide who was sent with the harp). At first, he looked very sad: His shoulders were slumped and he was bent forward, which suggested the weight of the *load* that the client was carrying. Then, the Indian guide stood up, straightened his shoulders, and folded his arms across his chest, which made him look strong and *sure* of himself.

I noticed a steel *rod* in his right hand, and I *asked* him about it. He answered:

> "It is what is inside this woman.
> She is strong enough to handle
> anything that comes her way. She is
> a very strong and capable person."

The Indian guide, then, turned around in a circle, which symbolized that the client's life would turn around. There would be *change*, and she would have the strength to disconnect from her mother (who had been a big issue with her). We, then, noticed *additional* Indians in the room, and they were dancing a dance called "A New Start."

I saw a former life of the client where all the family-members were present, and they happened to be the same family-members as the ones whom she had in her *current* life. They were all Native Americans, and her mother was as confused *then* as she *currently* was. And she was pushing out her daughter's *father* and bringing in *another* man. There was much fighting and hollering, all struggling for attention. I could see that the client's family-problems of her *current* life were the same as those in her *past* life.

I have seen many lifetimes that can come-and-go with the same people. And those people never seem to overcome their issues; they just keep dragging them into another time and place. Apparently, there had been no progress in their souls' evolution.

In any event, the client told me that growing up in her house was like being in a torture-chamber. There was no love or caring; there was only pushing, bickering, fighting, loud voices, and no consideration for anyone.

She had a desire to be with her father in her *past* life as she did in her *current* life. And similarly, her father was a child molester in her *past* life as he was in her *current* life: No improvement in his soul at all.

Then, I saw the eerie *truth* about her: She had a desire to be with her father in her *current* life because she, in a *former* life, had been his *wife* instead of his *daughter!* Hence, I then understood the very deep and strong Karmic *connection* that she had with her (current) father. I could see that she wanted *reconciliation* with her father, but she didn't know what *level* that he was in (concerning child molestation).

I, then, saw *another* former life of the client. This time, she was the daughter of the same woman who was her mother in her *current* life. She lived in the early 1800's, and her mother had birthed her out of wedlock. And unfortunately, the mother couldn't deal with the situation: The baby was only two days old, and the mother couldn't take care of her. Therefore, the mother placed the baby in a basket and took her to an orphanage.

Consequently, at the beginning of her former life, when she was taken to the orphanage as a baby, a large root of *rejection* entered the client's soul. The baby knew that, even though she was so young, she was "unwanted." In a sense, the mother was *pushing her away*, and the baby *felt* it.

I told the client that her spiritual wound would be *healed* before the session was over. At the orphanage, the girl had found a *dog* to love, which became her best friend, and it was true in her *current* life as well.

Then, I saw a wonderful thing. A group of *angels* appeared with a *stretcher*, and I asked:

"What are you doing?"

They replied:

"We're here to carry out the dead *body* that she has shed during the session."

I saw a black form that was the same size and shape of the client, and the angels lifted it off her and placed it on the stretcher and carried it away. The black form was the client's old body of thoughts, ideas, hurts, and fears that had accompanied her. She now would receive something brand new. And she immediately felt her mind and shoulders become lighter and lighter.

The client had come in looking dark in her face, bent over with burdens, and troubled about many things. And she went out lighter, walking so straight, and had so much more joy and peace. That is what kept me going with my work. The transformations in people's lives (in such a short period) were miracles, and I was so *privileged* to have been a part of it. The Bible tells us that it is by their fruits, you will know them.

Chapter 13: Case 4 -- Another Session, Another Truth

This case was a woman in her 50's who had a sister and a brother, and she had been in my life for many years.

At the time, I was regularly providing therapeutic massage to her in my home, and she always had a problem with her right shoulder. No matter how much I would treat it, it never seemed to be enough.

One day, I massaged her and spent an extra 30 minutes on the right shoulder. And as I was working, I had a *vision* as to why her shoulder was such a problem. I don't know how many people have ever heard of "karmic wound." It is a pain or a problem in our *current* life that has been carried over from a *former* life.

In my vision, I saw the client and her (current) sister living as members of the Cherokee Nation during the 1700's, but her (current) sister was a *brother* in the 1700's. Anyway, they were in a field together, and the client was shot-and-killed by her brother's arrow. She was only 18 years old when she was killed by the arrow that had gone through the right shoulder and had penetrated the right lung.

Incidentally, both her *current* family-members were the same as her *former* family-members, and her former family-members were all very *jealous* of her because of her ability to do beautiful beadwork.

After the vision, I never again wondered why she had so much trouble with her right shoulder.

This client came to me many times for various kinds of treatments. And I managed to help her to some degree, but she continued to have huge rejection-issues. I did every kind of therapy on her that I could. I repeatedly *prayed* for her and I weekly spent many hours on the *phone* with her, but she failed to carry out the instructions that she received. And therefore, to this day, her condition has remained the same.

Chapter 14: Cases 5,6,7

14a: Spiritual Surgery

This case was a married woman who was somewhere between 30 and 40 years old. She had been married two times, and she was amiable, co-operative, and very interested in my line of work.

We went through the usual discussion, applying the oils, praying, and checking the chakras. And during the Indian Harp procedure, a very interesting thing happened to her; and thereafter, it would happen to a few *other* clients.

She was relaxed and in a meditative state, and the Indian guide (who was sent with the harp) appeared. He had come to perform spiritual *surgery* on the client's head. She had a lot of dark thoughts, which were caused by her feeling of *guilt* for the two failed marriages, along with *other* bad things as well. The Indian guide removed the top of the client's head and began to pick out things that looked like *worms*, which were the thoughts that *troubled* her. He, then, replaced the top of her head.

It sounds crazy, but the Indian guide's procedure worked. From that day forward, the client was much better.

14b: Free Will

I witnessed a *similar* spiritual procedure as the one above. I had a vision over a woman who was 40 or 50 years old. And I saw the Indian guide remove the top of her head. But in *her* case, her thoughts were like a hill of *termites*, and they were running *everywhere* inside her mind. The Indian guide explained that termites eat wood, and they could destroy an entire *house* if they were permitted to multiply.

As mentioned earlier, the Bible reads:

> "Wisdom hath builded her house,
> she has hewn out her 7 pillars:"
> (Proverbs 9:1)

> Know ye not that ye are the temple
> of God, and that the Spirit of God
> dwelleth in you?" (1 Corinthians
> 3:16)

Many years ago, when I was studying the Tabernacle of Moses, I learned that wood is likened to (or, a type of) *humanity*.

Therefore, when I saw that the client's thoughts were like *termites*, and termites eat *wood*, and the client was the *house*, I realized that I was seeing a deep truth. And the truth was a revelation about the power of *thoughts*, and if we let them run *wild*, they will destroy us both in the *spiritual* and in the *physical.* It all made sense to me, for I have been coming into these deeper truths for many years.

Anyway, the Indian guide removed a lot of the thoughts (represented by the termites), but there were more in the foundation that could not be removed by him at the time. It would be up to *her* to spend the time to send light into those darker recesses of her mind and remove the remaining thoughts to a place where they could be destroyed. And I could *see* why the Indian guide could not remove the remainder of the offending thoughts: Her *free will* was blocking his attempt to improve her mental and physical health. I prayed *much* for the client after she left, for I stopped the treatment shortly after.

14c: Depression

One of my clients was a middle-aged, highly educated woman who had many problems; and her *biggest* problem was *depression.*

92

I treated her for eight months and managed to free her from the depression that had plagued her for so many years. And I give all the credit to the Spirit and to the client: The Spirt led each session, and the client faithfully obeyed the Spirit's instructions.

A very interesting thing happened during the client's treatment. During the sessions, her *husband's* spirit was released from an earthbound place so that it could ascend and go on.

During one session, I saw (in a vision) many people outside the window who either had passed over or *about* to pass over. They were standing and looking in; and they were asking:

> "When will it be *our* turn to ascend?
> Help us, *please.*"

This happened in 2010 during the time of the Haiti earthquake. The spirits had black faces, and their physical bodies were still undiscovered under the rubble. Their loved ones were holding them earthbound by their desire to keep them alive, which was an awesome truth to me.

We must *release* our loved ones if we want them to go on. There are *things* that they need to do on the other side. And we can *prevent* their ascent by our *clinging* to them; and the big thing is our keeping the *stuff* that they owned. "Release" is the name of progress.

In any event, during one of our sessions, the client and I made a good connection as usual, and a *truth* (that I never had *thought* of) came out.

Before the procedure of the harps, the client mentioned an *aunt* who was *unfriendly* toward her; the aunt was even hostile toward one of her own *sons*. And the son was so *good* to her. He would come to her whenever she needed anything; he would call her all the time; and he would pay her bills. He would tend to *so many* details, even though he lived many miles away. She, his own *mother*, treated him *badly* instead of being thankful or being appreciative, and she would constantly put him down and be *rude* to him.

When I put the Indian Harp on her, I suddenly had a vision: The aunt and her son had been *husband* and *wife* in a former life, and she had treated him the same in her *former* life as she did in her *current* life. The *situation* had changed, but the *pattern* had *continued*.

After the session, I could see this pattern in *other* clients who would come to me for treatments. It does explain *so much* in some peoples' lives.

Incidentally, this type of thing happened to *me* one day. My husband and I were living in an apartment that was in an old farm house which had been remodeled to create three apartments. We had lived in it for about two years, and we had been *shopping*. And as we were entering the driveway, I had a vision, and the whole scene in the natural dropped away like a veil: My husband and I were in a different lifetime. My current husband was my *brother*, and he was repairing a wagon wheel in the backyard in front of a huge barn.

Today, there is no structure anywhere near the apartment house, but the apartment house is on a foundation that is 200 years old. Therefore, it is very possible that we were brother and sister on the farm in a former life.

Anyway, as to the client, during a different session, her husband's *spirit* appeared and asked for forgiveness for his indiscretions when he was alive. She replied:

"I forgive you."

I, then, had a vision: The husband had come back in New York to an Irish Catholic family as a *boy*. And every time that the client would come for a treatment, the boy's spirit would appear at an older age as if he were growing up. And before long, the boy's spirit had grown into an adult spirit, and he continued to appear during the sessions.

We asked God's Spirit:

> "How can this be? Can he be in New York as a *child* and simultaneously be here with us as an *adult*?"

God's Spirit answered:

> "Yes, for we are all multi-dimensional."

The word "multi-dimensional" is a big word that simply means multi- (many) and dimensional (bodies). Or, many-bodies. (Webster's New World

Dictionary of the American Language, Copyright 1968.)

Here is a truth that concerns me personally, though it may be difficult to believe. I had a vision that involved my own father. As I mentioned earlier, he died many years ago, but his spirit is still around me every day. Sometimes I feel *less* of his presence, and at other times I feel *more* of his presence.

Anyway, approximately eight years ago, the Spirit told me that my father's spirit would enter a physical body again. He would be born in Oregon, and he would come back as a *boy* again. He would love the same things that he had loved when he was my father before he died. For example, he loved working with wood; he loved his tools; he was good at repairing engines; and he was incredibly neat.

I never told a *soul* about the vision. Then, several years later, my husband and I went to a garage sale. And I came across a box that contained many things that interested me, so I purchased it.

When we got home, I began to go through the items that were in the box, and I was pleasantly surprised to find a *sticker* that read "Oregon." I knew that it was the *Spirit* confirming to me the secret that I had kept for eight years.

I pondered over the occurrence for several days. And *since* then, I have had visions of my father's spirit in the physical body of a small child in *Oregon*, finding some sticks and trying to nail them together.

What a wonderful thing it is to know that we have many opportunities to come back and "get things right." We have many chances to overcome all the nasty things that we think, do, and carry out.

Chapter 15: Case 8 -- One Last Truth

I want to close with this wonderful case. I had a lovely lady client who was in her 50's, and I would treat her three or four times a year.

She worked in the educational field, and she was open-minded and open-spirited who knew much about the "Great Spirit" (as the Native Americans call it).

We had delightful times whenever she would come, and we learned so much, for she had a *capacity* to see spiritually.

One day, she arrived *early* for her session, and she said:

"I know that a group of *spirits* came with me today."

I asked:

"Do you know who they are?"

She replied:

"No, I don't. But I know that, during the *harp* procedure, we will find out."

We entered the therapy room and began the harp procedure. And as I was working with the Indian Harp, I suddenly saw all the spirits of the people who had come with her: They were all *her* spirits! Every spirit was herself in a past life that had been revealed (by the Spirit) during our visits! Now, that is *multi-dimensional!* We were so *amazed* at the truth that we both had seen. The Spirit was so *wonderful* to unveil so many deep things to us.

I have *retired* from doing the therapies, but I can honestly say that I do *miss* it a lot. I still see many things by the Spirit, and I have *visits* from loving spirits. They do not frighten me at all, for I know them and I love them. And I share the *messages* that I receive from them with their loved ones who are still living, and they (the living) are always so *grateful*.

Incidentally, I once had a special experience with a loving spirit. One of my clients had an aunt who was almost blind and becoming very frail. And one evening, I accompanied the client to sit for her aunt who, by now, was dying in a nursing home.

We tried to speak *softly*, but we evidently were still too loud. Therefore, the aunt would *moan*, from time to time, as a hint for us to be quiet. And finally, I said:

"I will leave and let her have
silence."

The aunt passed away shortly after at the age of
102-½, and of course, my husband and I attended the
funeral.

Whenever I attend funerals, I often see the
spirit of the deceased, and the funeral of the client's
aunt was no exception. I saw the aunt's spirit in front
of the casket, which had been brought to the church
that she had attended. And she was so *impatient* with
the whole affair. She kept saying:

"Hurry this thing up. I am anxious
to get on with the next step."

She also would motion her hands as if she were
saying:

"Speed it up, please."

She had been rather *feisty* when she was alive,
and I could see that she was the same even in death.

She visited me two or three years later during a deep sleep. She pinched my toes and woke me up.

I said:

> "Leave me alone and let me sleep.
> What do you want?"

She said:

> "You annoyed me with your talking
> to my niece, and so I likewise am
> annoying *you*."

I, then, *apologized* to her for disturbing her when she was dying at the nursing home, but she still would not leave. She just seemed to want to hang around, for the spirits know that the living can see and hear them.

I asked:

> "What do spirits *hate*?"

She answered:

"We hate *incense*. If you want to drive us out, burn *incense*."

I then asked:

"Are you happy?"

She replied:

"Of course!

Also, all the spirits whom I've ever met, have told me the same thing: They can do very *nicely* without all the nonsense of funerals. They are for the *living*, not the *dead*. Even my *own* funeral was a pain in the neck. But I expect the ritual to continue, for those who remain need *closure*. But for those who have passed on, it is so much better to just do what is *necessary*, for they are in a *hurry* to "get the show on the road."

She returned a year later just to say "hello," and

I haven't seen her since.

I pray that I have been used as a tool to confirm something *important* in the reader's life. Also, I hope that I have successfully informed the reader that the loved ones on the other side are very *involved* in our lives, and they *do* have things to tell us. I am so grateful, every day, for my father's spirit who looks after me along with many others. I thank the Creator for all that I have learned and for the privilege of working with the beautiful harps. I still feel the presence of Angel Aquarius and Angel Aurelia, and I remember well the *love* that they poured on everyone.

The great chiefs of old in the Native American tribes were such a wonderful education for me. I can still see them, and how *glorious* their headdresses were as they appeared to me. Thank you, thank you. I learned so much; and yet, it was just a drop in the ocean of mysteries of all that there is to learn. I love the mysteries of the spirit world, and I always will.

Chapter 16: Past Life Regression

While the Spirit of God was leading me into Vibrational Sound Therapy, He also was leading me into the technique called "Past Life Regression." I had read some books on the topic in the past, for I have *always* been interested in the human mind and the mind's ability to retain so much. And yet, we only remember things in the present moment. The Creator has blessed us with so much uniqueness in every part of our being, and the mind is one of the greatest mysteries, even to the many who have studied it at great length. The only way I know anything is because of God's Spirit. It is the Spirit that caused me to be so *curious* about so many things and to be open to searching out answers.

In all my years of working with the harps and doing the Vibrational Sound Healing, I used Past Life Regression at least 12 or 15 times with some very difficult cases. I only used it when *God's Spirit* would lead me, and He only would lead me when the client and I would reach an *impasse* in the healing-process.

This happened on occasion, and I would ask the clients if they were willing to have me regress them back to a former life. And if they said "Yes," I would ask the Spirit to lead me every step of the way. To regress means to "go back." *Past life Regression* means to return to a former life in the consciousness, to bring a healing to a situation or blockage in the *current* life. Many times, a rejection, a failed marriage, or a deep wound of some kind in a *former* life would show up as a major blockage in the *current* life.

I have witnessed healings take place through this therapy, and the healing *never* would have happened any other way.

I sometimes knew (by the Spirit of God) that the answer to a client's healing lay in a past life, and the healing would not have been possible any other way. The client had to be100% in favor of the treatment. Otherwise, it would not work at all.

I had many clients tell me that they wanted to be healed of certain things, and they knew that their problem(s) had originated very long ago in another lifetime. But then, when I would begin to regress them to a former life, *fear* would come in and cause them to stop the process.

I always would know if a client were not capable of going all the way to total healing, and so I sometimes would stop the entire process myself before the client would.

People want to get well, but they often don't want to face up to the very problem that needs to be remedied. Many clients would arrive at the very step of decision and then stop the treatment.

I never belittled anyone for stopping the treatment. I just let them know that God never goes against our free will. He gave us the free will, and we can use it in any way that we so desire. I also let them know that there would be no condemnation on them for leaving the process of regression. I just kept letting them know that they were loved, no matter what.

Usually, a session would require at least three hours, and many times, four hours or more. I never watched the clock, because in the spirit world, there is no time. I would keep going as long as I felt that the client was receiving a healing. I never charged for time. I would set a price, and the clients were happy to pay the small amount that I asked, for they knew that they would be helped.

I give all the praise to our great heavenly help who appeared during each session and gave me so completely the instructions that I needed to help a client who needed healing.

What if all this should happen to each of *us*?

It just might if we are open enough to allow the "Creator of all" to open our eyes. And we will be secure if we are aware of all the helpers who are around us. We are never alone!

Open the understanding, oh Creator, of all who read these words!

Amen.

Watch for my next book titled *Songs, Poems, and Musings*.